AF377684

THE ESSENCE OF

ARMANI

UNFOLDED

CONTENTS

The Beginning of
ARMANI

GIORGIO ARMANI IS A LEGEND in the fashion world. As the head fashion designer of his own brand until his death at age 91 in 2025, he managed to make the luxury house of Armani one of the most sought-after brands in the world.

ecades of the most important fashion innovations and looks came out of his skilled hands. He is easily one of the most widely recognized names in fashion, up there with Oscar de la Renta, Coco Chanel, Christian Dior, and Ralph Lauren. His influence and passion are carried on in the next generation with young designers taking inspiration from his many glamorous looks.

His looks were known to be minimalist, with staples that were the utmost in sophistication. The jackets and suits that he did were next-level extraordinary. The Armani suit is one of the most well-known pieces in fashion, worn by world leaders, celebrities, and billionaires, as well as the average man who wanted the absolute best suit possible to make the right impression.

So where did this powerhouse in fashion come from? And how did he manage to create a billion-dollar business on the back of an unstructured jacket coming from a tiny Italian town? It all started when he was born July 11, 1934, in Piacenza, Italy. His parents were Ugo Armani, who was an accountant by profession for a company that provided transportation, and his mom was Maria Raimondi. It's been said that his mother influenced his love for elegance and style.

HIS LOOKS WE
TO BE MINIMA
TABLE STHAT
WORN BY WOR
CELEBRITIES,
IRES AS WEL

FAMILY
*Giorgio Armani with his
siblings, Rosanna and
Sergio.*

ARMANI WAS A MIDDLE CHILD, growing up with an older brother
named Sergio and a younger sister named Rosanna. The family was
not well off, and growing up during World War II, he experienced a
lot of poverty and struggle as a child. Tragedy struck when he was
playing with an undetonated artillery shell that severely injured him
and also killed one of his young friends. This incident is probably
why, after high school, he decided to go into medicine at the Univer-
sity of Milan, where he studied for three years before joining the Italian army. Luckily, due to his medical background, he was assigned to
a military hospital in Verona where he was able to be exposed to the
fashion and culture the city had to offer. This was where he attended
his first fashion shows, which piqued his interest in another lifestyle.
In 1957, after two years in the military, he got a job as a window dresser and salesman at a famous department store in Milan called La Ri-
nascente. That led to working in the menswear department, which is
where his early sense of men's suits and fashion comes from. In the
mid-60s, he went to work for Nino Cerruti, who was a famous designer at the time. He designed menswear and learned from Cerruti
as his apprentice for over 10 years, all the while designing for different companies in a freelance capacity. It was years of intensive work
that laid the foundation for his skills in developing his own fashion
line in 1975.

HE WAS ONLY ABLE TO START his own line with the support of Sergio Galeotti, who would become his personal and professional partner for many years. Galeotti helped to finance Armani's line in July of 1975, presenting his first ready-to-wear men's collection in 1976 under his own name. Armani was already a darling with the press since his work was recognized for the many different fashion houses before his own that he put his stamp on.

The good news for women is that he also produced a ladies' line that same year. The 70s were an important time for the growth of the Armani brand. He was able to partner with Gruppo Finanzario Tessile, which made it possible to produce luxury couture and ready-to-wear items, as well as expand the brand into swimwear, accessories, and undergarments.

The 80s brought even more expansion to the budding Armani empire, when he was able to partner with L'Oreal to produce high-end perfumes and cosmetics. It was at this time that Emporio Armani came out, along with a denim line and Armani Junior. Clearly, Armani had his pulse on the world of fashion with a global brand that was coveted by just about everyone.

ven though he produced a lot of couture and luxury ready-to-wear, Armani understood the love for his brand, which is why he created AX Armani Exchange, a more casual line of affordable, everyday clothing that catered to the younger generation who couldn't afford a $5,000 suit or a priceless couture dress.

In his personal life, Armani never had any children. He was very close to his brother and sister's families, especially his nieces Silvana and Roberta Armani, and his nephew Andrea Camerana. His sister's elegance and beauty were always a factor in his designs since he considered her his muse. Each of these family members has always been closely involved in his brand throughout its inception and in keeping it flourishing throughout the decades.

His partner in business and life, Sergio Galeotti, passed away in 1985 from complications of AIDS. Armani always considered this one of the saddest parts of his life, that he wasn't able to prevent his passing.

SERGIO GALEOTTI AND GIORGIO ARMANI

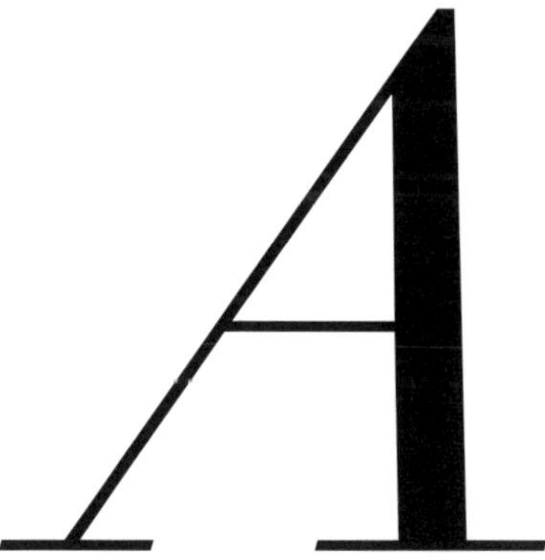

rmani's own health was strong right up until the end. He was 91 when he passed away on September 4, 2025. It was the first time that he missed one of his runway shows at Milan Fashion Week in June 2025. At the time that he died, it has been estimated that he was worth 12.1 billion dollars. His public memorial service was held at the Armani Teatro in Milan and was attended by 15,000 people. Later, he was buried in a private family ceremony at his family's burial plot in his hometown of Piacenza.

The succession plan for the company was of the utmost importance to Armani. It's now owned by the Giorgio Armani Foundation, with heavy involvement and ownership rights going to his family and his partner, Leo Dell'Orco.

"HE'S MANAGED
TO SELL
AMERICAN
CLOTHES
OF THE THIRTIES,
FORTIES, AND
FIFTIES,
*THAT GREAT
HOLLYWOOD LOOK*,
BACK TO THE
AMERICANS,
WHO THINK
THEY'RE
BUYING ITALIAN."

Eric Clapton in Vogue

ARMANI'S RIGHT-HAND MEN *AND HIS NIECES*

SINCE ARMANI WAS ALWAYS THE HEAD DESIGNER of his own brand and all of its entities, it's unlike many other brands that have multiple head designers. It's not that Armani didn't have assistance, because it would be impossible to run a multi-billion-dollar empire without a lot of people by his side. You could call these people his right-hand men. One of the most instrumental people in Armani's success was his business partner and close collaborator, Sergio Galeotti.

e was born in 1945 and by profession was an Italian architect and considered the co-founder of Armani. He and Giorgio Armani met in Tuscany in 1966. He was the finance brain and handled a lot of the administrative aspects of the growing fashion brand when it was created in 1975. It's been said that the two men started the brand with the sale of Armani's Volkswagen for a mere $700. The fact that a billion-dollar brand came from less than $1,000 really speaks to the genius and influence that Galeotti had on the business.

His personal relationship with Armani, along with their professional partnership, really served as the backbone for the company, leading to its success over those first 10 years. Armani has always said over the years that it was Galeotti's support and belief in him that led to the confidence he had to create and make the fashion empire what it is today. Without Galeotti by his side, Armani might never have created his iconic brand at all.

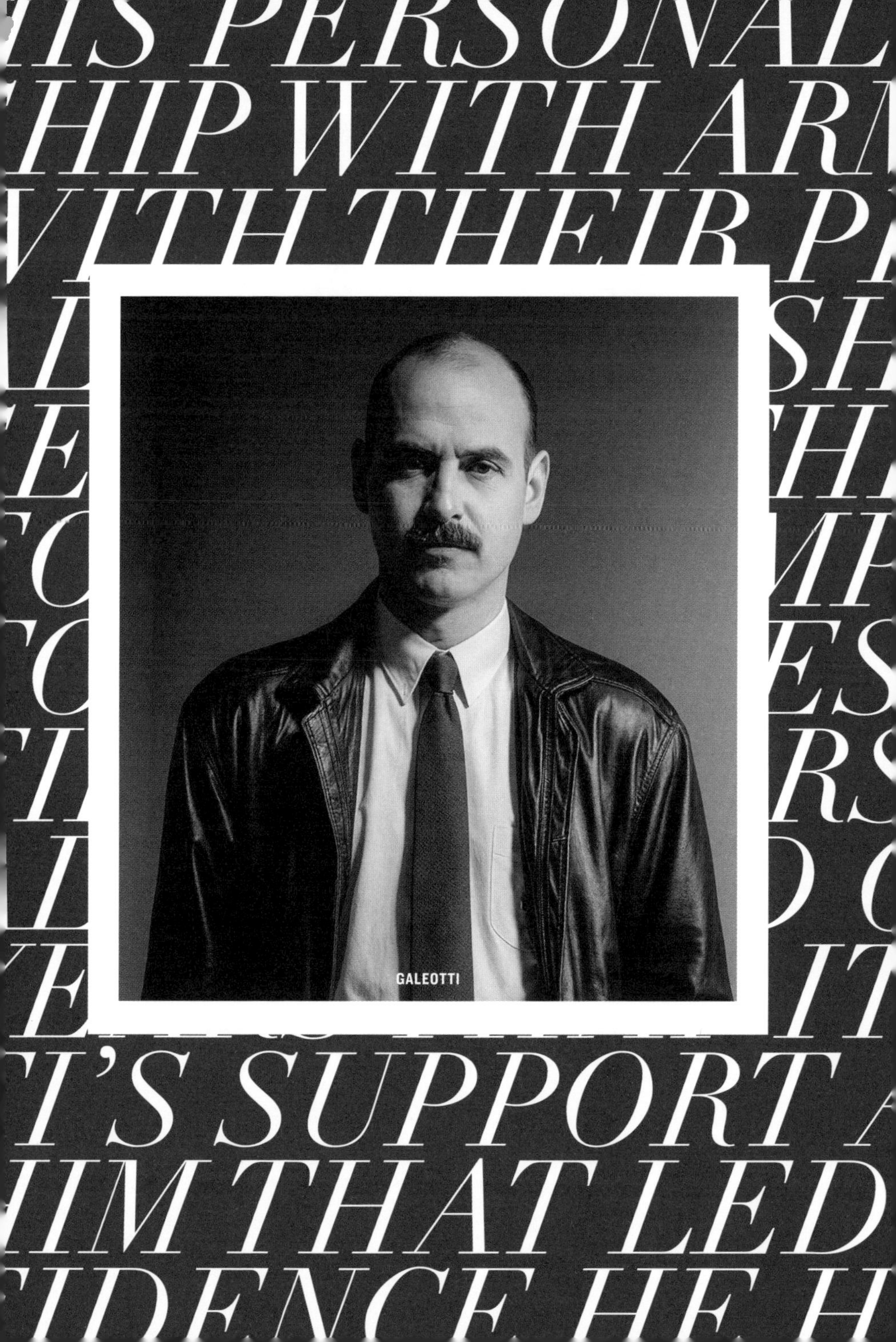
GALEOTTI

WHEN GALEOTTI passed away from complications of AIDS in 1985, it was a turning point for Armani. He once said that "Sergio made me believe in myself; he made me see the bigger world." After he was gone, Armani was at the height of success with his company and kept going in part due to his desire to honor Galeotti.

After Galeotti passed away, the next person who would serve as one of Armani's top advisors and collaborators would be Pantaleo Dell'Orco. He was born in the province of Bari, Italy, in 1952. He was originally the head of the men's style division and was close with Armani for over 45 years. Armani affectionately called him Leo, and even though he wasn't free with the compliments over the years, Dell'Orco knew what he meant to Armani.

Dell'Orco joined the Armani company in 1977, just two years after its inception. Armani used him as a model in the beginning. At the time, the company was operating out of Armani's apartment with just four desks. He had met Armani in the early 70s while walking his dogs at a park in Milan. After Sergio died, he quickly became one of Armani's most trusted confidants and an important part of the company, even though, for the most part, they kept their personal and professional relationship very private.

During Armani's life, Dell'Orco was always present at his fashion shows and press events right by his side. He ran all the men's collections, including Emporio Armani and Armani Exchange, as well as the main menswear for Giorgio Armani. When Armani wasn't able to attend one of his fashion shows in June 2025 due to illness, it was the first one he didn't attend. When interviewed at the show, Dell'Orco said that Armani was watching via a live stream and hated to miss it. Even though the two never married officially, it was known that Armani wore a ring that Dell'Orco had gifted to him, and they lived together.
After Armani's passing, Dell'Orco, through his will, is an important part of the succession plan the brand has going forward.

But it's not all men that run Armani. His two nieces have been important parts of the fashion organization. Those women are Silvana Armani and Roberta Armani. They are both the daughters of Armani's brother Sergio. They, along with Leo Dell'Orco, are considered the guardians for the future of Armani.

SERGIO'S DAUGHTER
Giorgio Armani and Roberta Armani at the 65th Festival de Cannes.

ilvana is on the board of Armani and considered the vice president of the brand, as well as the head of the women's divisions for Giorgio Armani, Emporio Armani, and Armani Exchange. She is seen as one of the creative and style forces that will carry on her uncle's legacy through her creativity. When she worked alongside Armani, she was able to learn how he liked his silhouettes and fabrics to be in each collection.

Her sister, Roberta, is the director and VP and head of public relations for the company. On an interesting note, one of her first jobs when she was younger was working at the Armani Exchange store in New York City, where she was raised.

She has the exciting task of overseeing celebrity relations for the brand and is known for her high-society connections from growing up as an Armani. Oftentimes, she has said that she was her uncle's favorite. She also holds a seat on the board, like her sister, and will be instrumental in continuing the success of Armani for the future.

"*A VISIONARY DESIGNER* WHOSE LEGACY WILL LIVE ON FOREVER. *I FEEL HONOURED TO HAVE CALLED HIM A FRIEND*"

ARMANI

THE HOTELS, MUSIC, *and* HIS SPORTS INTERESTS

NOT ALL OF GUCCI'S STORY IS ABOUT FLOWER PRINTS, gorgeous clothes, and pretty logo handbags; there is a sordid tale of murder and mayhem that happened within the Gucci family during the 90s. It was pretty shocking, to say the least. So, what happened all those years ago that brought a true-crime angle to the House of Gucci?

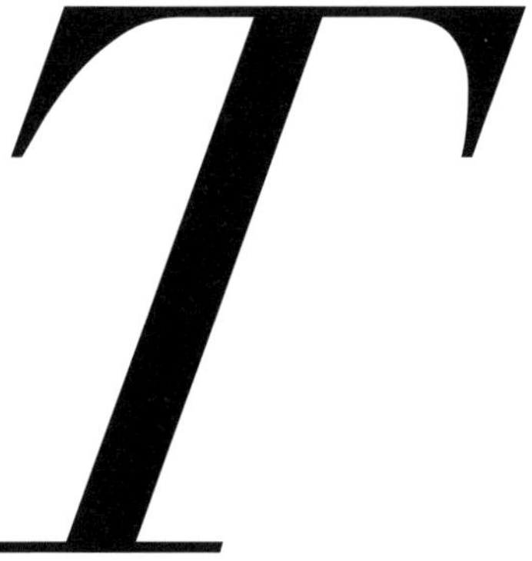

here are lots of interesting things going on in the Armani sphere of interest that don't have anything to do with fashion. Most of those things have to do with his hotels, his music, and his sports interests. He was really able to translate interest in the Armani brand into a variety of profitable ventures that got the name of the brand out into the public eye even more than it already was with just the clothing alone. One that does have to do with fashion is his work in the film industry with costuming.

HERE ARE LOT
STING THINGS
THE ARMANI
ATE INTERES
NI BRAND INT
DE PROFITABL

HOLLYWOOD CALLS *FOR ARMANI SUITS*

AMERICAN GIGOLO was one of those films that Armani was involved with that came out in 1980. Armani felt that his work in the film industry was a boon to his brand, both for creativity and keeping his clothing in a worldwide spotlight. This is a film that starred Richard Gere as a high-end escort named Julian who lived a lavish lifestyle. The film also starred the gorgeous Lauren Hutton, whom Armani was very close to. One of the most famous scenes in the film is where Gere's character rips open his dresser with a bounty of perfectly folded Armani shirts. Armani himself created four beautiful suits that the character wore in various scenes, looking like the perfect movie star.

Since this film came out only five years after Armani started his company, it really helped to get his name out there in the luxury design world. This first film led to Armani designing for over a hundred films in the Hollywood industry. Another important film that Armani did the suiting for was the movie The Untouchables. This was a 1987 crime drama that starred Robert De Niro, Kevin Costner, and Sean Connery. Having these powerful men in the film wear Armani suits became an important part of film and fashion history.

AMERICAN GIGOLO

Richard Gere in Armani in the hit movie American Gigolo.

THE UNTOUCHABLES

Kevin Costner stars as Eliot Ness, anchoring The Untouchables with restraint, moral resolve, and authority.

ERIC CLAPTON
AND ARMANI

ANOTHER INTERESTING collab that Armani had was with musician Eric Clapton. In the 90s, Clapton composed songs for Armani's runway shows. They became quite good friends through the years. Plus, he was often dressed by Armani for red carpet events and award shows. He also helped Armani open two Emporio Armani stores in New York City, and Armani hosted an event for Clapton when he auctioned off some of his Crossroads guitars for charity. The charity was for the Crossroads Center in Antigua, a residential treatment center for drug and alcohol addiction that Clapton started in 1998. The money from the auction helped to subsidize treatment for those who couldn't afford it. Other famous musicians also donated guitars that they had used at the Crossroads Guitar Festivals.

ARMANI BANS SUPER SKINNY MODELS

IN 2006, after the death of model Ana Carolina Reston from anorexia, Armani made it a priority to ban overly skinny models from his runway shows and ads. This was a common problem in the fashion and modeling industry, with some of the models having an unhealthy body weight. He was adamant that his models be healthy and wanted to get past the industry's obsession with hyper-thin models. This type of figure isn't realistic for the majority of women in the world, and Armani understood that, which was very unusual.

Although even with this mandate in place, he was criticized over the years for having models that were too thin on his showroom floors and on the runways. It was a hard standard to maintain in an industry that clamored for stick-thin women. When asked why this happened, he always put the blame on the stylists and the public who liked to see those very thin frames. Overall, he did try to make sure that all of his models had a body mass index of at least 18.

THE
HOTELS

HOTELS WERE ANOTHER AREA of hospitality that Armani got into in 2005 when he signed an agreement with Emaar Properties. This was with the goal of building a series of luxury hotels and resorts under the Armani brand name. The first Armani Hotel opened up in 2010 at the Burj Khalifa in Dubai, United Arab Emirates, and it to this day is a magnificent property to visit.

The hotel itself featured 160 guest rooms and 140 permanent residences that were decked out in full Armani Casa splendor. This included furnishings and floral arrangements from Armani Fiori that were the pinnacle of grand design.

A second Armani hotel didn't open up until 2011, which was fittingly in Milan, in an exclusive location right in the heart of the city. It's a five-star hotel with a spa, the Armani Ristorante, and gorgeous ballrooms for events. For both of these hotels, Armani took a hands-on approach in his design work, overseeing almost all aspects of their creation. The details in each room and throughout the properties are thoughtful and gorgeous. The logo is present on many of the décor and furnishings, making these hotels a true tribute in life-size form to the Armani brand.

Italy

SPORTS
INTERESTS

ARMANI WAS A HUGE SPORTS FAN. He loved basketball, which included the Olimpia Milano basketball team, and was often seen at games courtside. In fact, Armani was such a fan of the team that he actually bought it in 2008 from Giorgio Corbelli and owned it until his passing. His ownership and support helped the team to be revived and more successful that they called it EA7 Emporio Armani Milan in his honor. As the sole owner, he was able to change up the management of the team, which led to them winning a lot more games. They won multiple Italian League Championships, Italian Cups, and SuperCups. Italy loved the fact that sport was combined with fashion in such a chic and cool way.

Soccer, or "football" as it's called internationally, was another love of his, with him throwing his support at Inter Milan and AC Milan.
He even designed the uniforms for England's national soccer team twice. He also designed suits worn by Chelsea FC, so that their team looked like dapper gentlemen heading into matches.
In the Olympics, he designed a couple of different things, including the flag bearers' outfits for Italy at the 2006 Olympics in Turin and the Olympic uniforms for Italy at the 2012 Olympics in London.

Racing was another sports industry that Armani designed for. He entered a multi-year partnership with Scuderia Ferrari and provided travel wear for the entire team. It easily became one of the most recognized partnerships with the motorsports company.

LEFI
RESS
icent
OF EVIL

"*KIND,
GENEROUS
AND LOYAL.*
A TRUE PIONEER
OF ELEGANCE.
*A GLOBAL
INSPIRATION.*"

The POWER SUIT *and Fashionable* STAPLES

GIORGIO ARMANI had amazing design knowledge. He is responsible for coming up with decades of luxurious fashion that broke the mold and was very ahead of its time each season. Overall, if you were going to describe what the clothing of Armani looked like, understated elegance comes to mind. Some of his best work revolved around unstructured suits that redesigned what menswear and womenswear should look like on a global stage.

HIS LINES WERE MINIMALIST, with luxury fabrics and an attention to detail unlike any other. The clothing someone bought from Armani would last a lifetime, meant to be worn again and again with the utmost quality. Some of the qualities of the deconstructed suits were gorgeous tailoring and a structure that provided both shape and comfort. He removed some of the restrictive shoulder pads that were such a part of the suiting industry. Heavy linings were also removed to make being able to move in his suits much easier. There was a pleasure in wearing an Armani suit. The lightweight construction and fluid drape made everything more seamless to wear.

THE MEN'S UNSTRUCTURED JACKET or BLAZER

DURING THE MID-70S when Armani created his line, men's jackets were stiff and uncomfortable to wear. Suits were more like armor than comfortable clothing. That's why, when Armani came out with his unstructured jacket or blazer, it was revolutionary. He completely redesigned the internal structure of the jacket, taking out that heavy lining and getting rid of the bulky shoulder pads that sometimes made men feel like a football linebacker, and not in a good way. He also changed where the buttons should be placed, making them lower, which added to the overall relaxed vibe and feel of the jacket when worn.

The high-end but lightweight fabrics that made up the jacket were materials like twist wool and linen blends, which had breathability and comfort. The man wore the suit instead of the suit wearing the man in many of Armani's exceptional jacket designs.

The WOMEN'S POWER PANTSUIT

ALTHOUGH WHEN YOU THINK of power pantsuit, Hillary Clinton comes to mind, it was Armani who made the women's power pantsuit a global fashion movement for women in the workforce. He was really the originator of getting the pantsuit on the red carpet when the great Diane Keaton wore his unstructured jacket in 1978 at the Academy Awards. When she walked the red carpet in that look and accepted her Oscar later that night, an extraordinary fashion moment was born. Politics was definitely a place where the Armani women's power pantsuit shined. Not only did Hillary Clinton rock this look, but so did Nancy Pelosi with her extensive collection of Armani pantsuits. Decades of Armani power suits have been worn all over the world by women in very important positions.

Minimalist EVENING GOWNS

ANOTHER BEAUTIFUL PLACE for Armani in legendary fashion were his red carpet looks in minimalist evening gowns. He knew that a gown didn't have to be overwhelming all the time to be beautiful. Stars throughout the years have worn his looks at events and award shows. The type of gown that Armani designed was meant to be fluid and comfortable. The tailoring and dramatic drape of each gown is meant to be memorable. That didn't mean there weren't intricate and expensive details on each dress, because there were, in materials like silk, tulle, and fine velvet. The colors ranged from rich jewel tones to black and neutrals that were anything but ordinary.

Some of the celebs who were known to wear Armani on the red carpet are Jodie Foster, Julia Roberts, Cate Blanchett, and Beyoncé. Stars young and established were always honored to be seen in an Armani gown.

Wide-Legged TROUSERS

Wide-legged trousers are characterized by being fitted at the waist and hips but gradually going down into a relaxed fit from mid-thigh to the ankle. They are meant to be more comfortable and fluid and can go with a variety of tops and jackets. The key was having a consistent relaxed fit from the hip down, so that these pants didn't end up looking too flared or like bell bottoms. Armani's wide-legged trousers had a relaxed ease and elegance to them. His brand still makes these pants today in a variety of fabrics meant to be comfortable and easy to wear.

KNITWEAR and CASHMERE

Beautiful sweaters and knitwear were a big part of Armani's lines throughout the years. The meticulous craftsmanship and elegant design of the knitwear meant that if you had one of these pieces from Armani, it was going to last for years. The cashmere especially was known for its softness and luxurious feel. People have described Armani cashmere as being like a wispy soft cloud.

Neutral COLORS

Armani really liked to use neutral colors in many of his designs. The reason that he did this was that he believed that the item's fabric and tailoring were the true stars of the show. He believed neutrals were the epitome of modern sophistication. Some of his favorite colors were beige, gray, and black to impart a sense of quiet luxury. One of his signature colors was something that he described as "greige." It's obviously a combination of gray and beige, but he felt that this neutral tone was truly something special and metropolitan.

Velvet PIECES

VELVET WAS ANOTHER MATERIAL that Armani used quite often in tuxedos for men and glorious evening gowns for women. This was especially true in 2006, when Armani ushered in a new era of velvet on the runways in beautiful jewel tones and deep-pile fabrics in everything from diamond-patterned velvet jackets to soft, cozy slippers. At the end of the show, Armani took his bow on the runway in a black velvet suit.

Velvet was incorporated with silks, velour, stripes, and tweeds. Even though it was very present that year as a velvet revolution, Armani has always done key pieces in velvet over the years. It's a standout material that, when done right, can be very elegant and expensive looking.

"SO MANY SIGNIFICANT MOMENTS IN MY LIFE, *AWARDS, WEDDING, WIMBLEDON ...ALL IN ARMANI"*

Russel Crove on X

WATCHES, JEWELRY, *and* ARMANI CASA

THERE ARE THREE MAIN LINES of Armani. They include Giorgio Armani, the original and most high-end of the brand. Then there is Emporio Armani, which is more accessible yet still luxurious and slightly more affordable. Finally, there is A|X Armani Exchange, which is a casual and affordable line. In all of these arms of the brand's reach, there are key pieces other than clothing. That includes things like watches, jewelry, and Armani Casa, their home collection. Let's look at some of the most important accessories that Armani makes along with their stunning home collection.

ARMANI

I/CASA

WATCHES

ARMANI ONLY STARTED to make watches in the 1990s. Its first watch was a casual one that appeared in the A|X Armani Exchange line. This was meant to be part of the cutting edge of fashion, with watches that were trendy but still elegant. The watches he came out with were a combination of Italian elegance with Swiss movement, and everyone knows that Switzerland makes some of the highest quality watches in the world. Even though the A|X Armani Exchange watches were designed and made in Italy, they featured that all-important Swiss movement.

Since they were designed for the Exchange line, Armani was able to feature more modern materials including silicone, stainless steel, and ceramic. Many of the pieces featured interchangeable designs where someone could swap out the straps or have different dial designs. The iconic A|X logo was always a key part of each watch, which meant that the wearer could proudly showcase that they shopped from the trendy A|X Armani Exchange store.

The watches were meant for everyday wear and were water resistant up to 50 meters, some even more, so these were very durable and lasting timepieces. Here are a couple of examples from the men's and women's collections.

A|X ARMANI EXCHANGE MEN'S BLACK STAINLESS STEEL *CHRONOGRAPH WATCH AX2716*

This watch combines luxury with functionality and features a 42 mm round stainless steel case and a sleek black dial. This timepiece showcases a chronograph display powered by a reliable quartz movement. The black stainless steel strap adds an extra layer of sophistication, secured with a sliding clasp. The watch also includes durable mineral glass. Perfect for casual occasions, this is a stylish and practical addition to anyone's collection.

A|X ARMANI EXCHANGE WOMEN'S TWO-TONE ANALOG *STAINLESS STEEL WATCH AX7156SE*

This is a stunning timepiece that blends elegance with modern style. The 36 mm round case is crafted from stainless steel, featuring a silver sunray dial with a three-hand quartz movement. Its two-tone stainless steel bracelet adds a touch of sophistication, secured with a foldover clasp with a push button for a secure fit. With 3 ATM water resistance and mineral glass, and being lightweight at just 75.5 g, it's an ideal accessory for any occasion. This set includes the watch and a stylish gold-tone bracelet, making it a perfect gift.

JEWELRY

THE HISTORY OF ARMANI making jewelry began in 2002 under the Emporio Armani line. It was a natural extension of the brand to make well-crafted but everyday jewelry pieces. The jewelry itself is meant to mimic the brand's clothing line: elegant and understated.

The fine jewelry collection came out in 2019 as part of the main Giorgio Armani line. He debuted the collection during Paris Haute Couture Week. This was a line of "high jewelry" that drew from historical elements the line had and key Armani design codes. The Blanche Collection featured the rare Arabian jasmine flower in 18K gold with white agate, peridot, and diamonds, of course.

Another important collection of high or fine jewelry that Armani did came out in 2022 called the Joséphine Collection. It was inspired by Joséphine de Beauharnais and featured chalcedony and gray diamonds. She was a French Empress who was the first wife of Emperor Napoleon I. The fine jewelry line was meant to be wearable even though it was crafted of the finest materials.

ARMANI CASA

IF YOU ARE A FAN OF ARMANI CLOTHING, then it's a natural extension to want to outfit your home in everything the man designed. The home décor and furnishings line was introduced by Armani in 2000. The first Armani/Casa store opened up in Milan, of course, with another one in the United States opening up soon after in New York City and Los Angeles. The line was meant to embody the spirit of Armani with elegance and grace, but also be comfortable and practical at the same time.

Understated luxury is what comes to mind when someone outfits their home in Armani/Casa. It's beautiful, but at the same time is meant to create a seamless and harmonious living space. The materials were always high quality with nods to Art Deco style and with pieces that were meant to be timeless.
One of the most important pieces forArmani/Casa was the Logo Lamp, which Armani created himself in 1982. The Logo Lamp obviously featured the Armani/Casa logo, but with a very simple design, it remains one of the most important pieces they make to this day. When he originally designed it, it was only because he needed a table lamp for his office in Milan on the famous Via Durini. It's a pretty straightforward lamp with a geometric pyramid shade and a slim stem and base. Chic. The shape has remained the same over the years with new materials making it unique. Elle Decor magazine featured the 2024 version of the Logo Lamp, which has walnut wood and a lacquered slatted lampshade.

"A GREAT HONOUR *TO HAVE HAD THE CHANCE TO MEET AND WORK WITH SUCH AN AMAZING PERSON.* YOU WILL BE MISSED GIORGIO. "

The LA PRIMA IS BORN *and* REBORN

IT'S NATURAL FOR ANY LUXURY DESIGN line to want to outfit their clientele head-to-toe. That includes having just the right handbag to make or break a look. Armani definitely knew that. He started to make handbags as part of his main line just four years after the brand launched, in 1979. It wasn't until 1994 that he started to produce more handbags after signing a partnership agreement with Redwall, which was an Italian leather company.

WHAT WAS CONSIDERED the first Armani signature handbag came out in 1995. Armani of course designed it himself, naming it La Prima or "the first." This iconic bag was modeled after an unstructured jacket, which was fitting as one of Armani's most important clothing pieces. He relaunched this bag in 2019 with modern updates and materials. It's a sleek handbag that can be worn over the shoulder or crossbody. Inside the bag there are three distinctive pockets, a mirror holder, and a lipstick case. So not only is this a truly chic bag, it's practical in many ways too. The leather material is soft calfskin, but some of the evening versions come in crocodile and lizard options, with the prices ranging from $12,000 to $13,500. The good news about this bag is that the style is casual enough for day but can transition into a night bag rather easily.

The relaunch in 2019 included six new bags: a classic model in two different sizes, two trunks, and two small shell clutches. There were 11 different colors that these bags came in, including white, ice, nude, leather, burgundy, dark brown, black, grass and military green, red, and powder blue. The La Prima handbag was sold in the main Giorgio Armani boutique stores.
There is an entire collection of handbags, including totes, shopping bags, backpacks, and mini bags in the main Armani line. There are also handbags that are exclusively made for Emporio Armani and the A|X Armani Exchange lines. There are many designs to choose from, but here are six of the most popular designs that everyone should consider owning.

Giorgio Armani
MYEA
SHOPPER BAG

This has gold-tone carabiner clips and tags featuring embossed logo lettering. The magnetic closure ensures essentials are secure while offering easy access when needed. Continuing with its functional appeal, the bag can be used as a shoulder bag, thanks to its beige detachable logo strap, or held by hand. Inside, a matching detachable pouch provides additional storage.

Giorgio Armani
DOUBLE-HANDLED SHOPPER BAG

This has a unique woven nappa leather-effect material in a soft lavender shade that evokes the calm of spring mornings. The bag draws inspiration from archival styles, reflecting Armani's ability to celebrate the past while adjusting to contemporary trends. This bag maintains its stylish ethos without compromising on function. The oversized structure provides ample space for daily essentials.

Giorgio Armani
MYEA BASKETWEAVE SHOPPER BAG

Giorgio Armani A bag that has a tactile basketweave design, adding a rustic charm that belies its high-fashion pedigree. The bag features two handles and a magnetic closure, reserving its loudest statement for functionality. Its logo snap hooks serve both as eye-catching hardware and practical adornment. Additionally, its removable webbing shoulder strap transforms it from a prim handbag to a convenient crossbody bag in an instant. Inside, an internal zipped pouch keeps your valuables safe and organized.

Giorgio Armani
HOBO BAG

A very cool bag that is made from bullskin, it is a tribute to the deconstructed suit jacket that first gave the brand its iconic status in high-end fashion. With a distinctive square shape, it's quite a departure from the typical hobo bags as it embraces the urban and free-spirited aesthetic of street fashion. It is made of soft suede leather in an appealing dark brown hue. Its magnetic closure keeps your essentials secure, and its interior is spacious enough to fit your everyday items.

Giorgio Armani
LA PRIMA SATIN MINI HOBO BAG

The iconic La Prima takes the simple structure of a hobo bag and gives it an evening-worthy upgrade, with its shimmering satin material and radiant all-over rhinestone appliqués. The bag's miniaturized form factor is a nod to the current trend of scaled-down accessories. The dazzling rhinestones set against the smooth satin material create a visual contrast, giving the bag an opulent texture that catches the light. The bag also provides functionality with its dual wearability. You can wear it as a tote with its removable rhinestone-covered handle with a snap hook, or sling it effortlessly across your body using the adjustable shoulder strap with stud-button fastening.

Giorgio Armani
BUCKET BAG

Giorgio Armani This features a supple structure that adheres to modern luxury sensibilities. The handle hole lends a unique touch while the chain shoulder strap adds a dash of metallic glint. The deer-print finish adds an extra layer of textural intrigue. Despite being a bucket bag, it doesn't fall short on organizational features. An accompanying internal zip pouch ensures your smaller essentials stay put. The bag also sports a silk-screen-printed logo.

"THOUGH HE WAS AN ICON OF THE WORLD OF FASHION, HE LIVED WITH GREAT HUMILITY AND A LOVE OF LIVING THAT INSPIRED THE WAY HE WORKED AND THE WAY HE LIVED. *HE CREATED A WORLD REFLECTING ALL THE THINGS HE LOVED* WITH A FOREVERNESS THAT WILL BE HIS LEGACY"

MOMENTS *Where* ARMANI *SHINED*

GIORGIO ARMANI was a legendary figure not only in the design world, but in the world of entertainment and pop culture.

E veryone has immediate recognizability with the name Armani, so it's natural that he would often make the news over the decades that he influenced the fashion industry and many others. The film industry with costume design was especially a bright light in Armani's life and legacy. Here are some more moments in the film industry where Armani made his mark and some other pivotal moments where his legendary status shined bright in pop culture.

HOLLYWOO D

MORE FILM MOMENTS

ARMANI'S WORK with men's costuming on-screen is nothing short of remarkable. He contributed costumes to over 200 films. It's well known that he did the suiting and shirts for Richard Gere's character in American Gigolo, but there are so many other iconic films that he worked on. Another one of the first films that he designed for was a horror movie called Phenomena, which starred Jennifer Connelly in 1985. She mostly wore white and oversized blouses, which was a sharp contrast to the violent nature of the film, making her look like the innocent young ingenue that she was.

Goodfellas was another stand-out costumed cast, with some of the stars who played famous gangsters in the movie wearing Armani suits. Armani himself didn't design the suits specifically for the film, but rather the costume designer Richard Bruno chose to use Armani suits on many of the characters. This Martin Scorsese classic came out in 1990. Another film that Armani did design for was Casino, in which the star Robert De Niro wore custom-designed Armani suits as Sam "Ace" Rothstein, the high-powered casino and hotel executive.

For the Boys was a film starring Bette Midler in 1991. Armani did the costumes for her character, with the female power pantsuit being center stage. The early looks in the movie were classic 80s power dressing, but softened over the decades the film took place. The entire wardrobe for the film really showed how versatile Armani was as a designer.

No one will forget the dashing Kevin Costner in the 1992 movie The Bodyguard. He wore custom-designed Armani suits while acting as the title bodyguard for Whitney Houston's pop star character. The suits in gray, navy, and charcoal were muted tones to act as a contrast for Whitney's superstar character and her more elaborate costumes. Either way, anytime you can see Kevin Costner in an Armani suit is well worth the price of admission.

MOVIE HITS
In Goodfellas, For the Boys, and The Bodyguard, Armani dressed the lead characters.

LADY GAGA AND ARMANI

He entered into a partnership with Lady Gaga to not only dress her on the red carpet, but he also did costumes for two of her world tours. Those included The Monster Ball Tour and the Born This Way Tour. Plus, at the Grammy Awards in 2010, Lady Gaga wore Armani Privé with a showstopping look that was a stunning silver masterpiece. This moment ushered in the era of Armani working with some of the hottest stars in Hollywood and the music industry.

GIORGIO ARMANI
MY WAY
THE REFILLABLE EAU DE PARFUM
MY WAY
GIORGIO ARMANI

ARMANI BEAUTY

IN 1980, Armani entered into an agreement with L'Oreal Beauty to make their fragrances and cosmetic products. The first products that the brand came out with were a women's and men's fragrance that launched in 1982 and 1984 respectively. They went on to develop a complete beauty and skincare line which featured celebs like Beyoncé, Cate Blanchett, Megan Fox, and Sydney Sweeney over the years.

Sydney Sweeney was a big get for the company, as she is one of the most popular young stars of today with roles in films like Anyone But You and TV shows like The White Lotus and Euphoria. She is considered a global fragrance and makeup ambassador for the company.

THE GREEN CARPET CHALLENGE

ARMANI WAS A HAPPY PARTICIPANT in The Green Carpet Challenge. This is an initiative that was founded by Colin Firth's wife, Livia Firth. The goal is to promote sustainable fashion. Armani was actually the first designer to participate in the challenge, which launched in 2011. He created both a sustainable evening gown and a custom tuxedo for the Firths. It used the red carpet as a platform for eco-friendly materials and design. The fashion was ethical and sustainable, but also high fashion and luxury, proving that sustainable design doesn't have to be drab and boring. The result was Italian craftsmanship combined with the best in sustainable ideas including the proper fabrics, renewable energy sources, and an eco-conscious design aesthetic.

HOLLYWOOD
FOREIGN
PRESS
ASSOCIATION
GOLDEN
GLOBE
DS
GOLD
GLO
AWA

THE GUGGENHEIM MUSEUM

IN CELEBRATION of 25 years of Giorgio Armani, the Guggenheim Museum in New York City put on a retrospective of his work in 2000. This was the first time the museum did an exhibit of a living designer. Over 200 garments, as well as different sketches and in-progress work, were on display in the Frank Lloyd Wright rotunda gallery.

Armani himself said when interviewed about the exhibit:

"The Guggenheim is without doubt one of the most important modern art museums in the world today, so it is a great honor to have had my work selected for an exhibition there in 2000. It is also very humbling to know that the Guggenheim has chosen my designs to stand alongside the work of some of the most influential artists of the 20th century, many of whom have been such a strong inspiration for me. Fashion is at the heart of human expression. It's a mirror that reflects society and culture. My philosophy has always been to help women and men feel comfortable and confident through the clothes that they wear, rather than to create decoration for the sake of it. The belief continues to be at the root of my work as we enter the new millennium."

> # *"HEARTBROKEN TO HEAR ABOUT THE PASSING OF A LEGEND. A TRUE MASTER OF HIS CRAFT."*

Cindy Crawford on Instagram

ARMARNI
from the 70s
TO TODAY

Famous Models

A BIG WIN for any model is to do high-end runway, couture, and editorial work for a famous design house.

G

iorgio Armani is one of those that has been at the forefront of fashion culture from the 70s to today. There are many famous models who have strutted the catwalks wearing the finest Armani suits and gowns the brand has to offer. These looks and the ads that have been done for everything Armani, including beauty and fragrance, have made the careers of many of these models and helped celebs reach the next level of fame. Here are some of the best Armani models and campaigns over the decades.

Gia CARANGI

A HUGELY FAMOUS MODEL who did Armani ad campaigns in the late 70s and 80s. The ads she did for Armani appeared in Vogue and other high-end fashion magazines. One of the ads was shot by photographer Aldo Fallai and was for Giorgio Armani's Spring/Summer 1980 collection. In the photos, she is in one of Armani's power suits for women, but the shoulders are relaxed and the look is rather androgynous. Armani wasn't the only luxury fashion house she modeled for. She was seen in Versace, Dior, and Yves Saint Laurent campaigns in the 80s before she tragically passed away from AIDS-related complications in 1986.

GIORGIO ARMANI

Bill QUINN

THE LADIES weren't the only famous faces for Armani. Bill Quinn was a male model who did some Armani campaigns in the 80s. He was in Armani's Fall/Winter 1985 editorial campaigns and was the epitome of the "Armani man" aesthetic of the mid-80s with relaxed tailoring, wide silhouettes, and a confident ease.

Burke HUDSON

This was another gorgeous male model that did editorial work for Armani. He was featured in the Armani Spring/Summer 1988 campaign. His work with Armani during the last part of the 80s made him a recognizable face for the fashion house.

—●—

Marcus HUDSON

He was a Swedish model who worked for Armani for quite a few years. While perhaps more strongly associated with the 1990s, his inclusion indicates Armani's roster of high-profile models spanned both the late 80s and beyond. One of his best campaigns was for the Armani Fall/Winter 1994 ads, where he was wearing the clothes but also modeled for the fragrance line.

—●—

Nadège DU BOSPERTUS

Another popular model in the 90s for the womenswear line was Nadège du Bospertus. She is credited with being one of Armani's favorite muses at the time. She appeared in advertising campaigns but also walked quite a few of Armani's runways.

—●—

Amber VALLETTA

Another super-watt supermodel in the 90s who modeled for Armani was Amber Valletta. She is listed as the model for the Armani Fall/Winter 1993 women's campaign. Peter Lindbergh was the photographer on that project. Some of the ads were in black and white, where she was shown with a male model, both wearing Armani menswear looks. The campaign's visuals contribute to Armani's early-90s power dressing with a luxury minimalism vibe that included strong silhouettes, refined tailoring, and a neutral palette with subtle sophistication.

Claudia SCHIFFER

ONE OF THE GREATEST supermodels of the 90s was x. Her icy blonde perfection was a perfect match with Armani's sleek and sexy evening gowns. When she showed up in any ad or on the runway, it was immediately known as an important fashion moment. One of her best moments in Armani was photographed by Arthur Elgort, which shows her in an off-white pantsuit featured in Vogue.

Kimora
LEE SIMMONS

SHE MODELED for Armani on the runways in the late 90s and early 2000s. In late 1998, Kimora married record producer Russell Simmons, so she mostly stopped modeling, but continued to wear Armani clothing on red carpets and for different events.

Other notable
2000S MODELS

There are many models over the past two decades who have done
runway shows and ads. Some of those models include

Erin O'CONNOR

Starred in the Women's Giorgio Armani Fall/Winter 2000 campaign.

Jessica STAM

Was in the Men's/Women's Giorgio Armani Spring/Summer 2007 Eyewear campaign along with male model Andy Richardson.

Raquel ZIMMERMAN

Did a few different campaigns for Armani during the 2000s.

Celebs

WHO HAVE MODELED IN BEAUTY AND FRAGRANCE

In the past few years, Armani Beauty and Fragrance has really upped their star power by hiring younger actresses who appeal to the next generation of Armani fans.

Tessa THOMPSON

In 2022, Armani Beauty named a global ambassador; she stars in campaigns for the brand's iconic Luminous Silk Foundation and Lip Power lines.

Hanni

A very cool K-pop singer, who was named global makeup ambassador for Armani Beauty and was featured in the "Power Fabric+ Foundation" campaign.

Sydney SWEENY

one of the most popular Gen Z actresses, who became an
ambassador for Armani Beauty in January 2023.

—●—

Nathalie EMMANUEL

Was appointed global makeup ambassador of Armani
Beauty in late 2024 and is featured in Luminous Silk
Foundation campaigns.

—●—

Sadie SINK

The actress who is famous for being on the Netflix hit
Stranger Things, who stars in Armani Beauty's
"Sì Passione Eau de Parfum Intense" campaign.

—●—

Sara SAMPAIO

A model and actress listed as a Giorgio
Armani Beauty ambassador.

Jamilla AWAD

A gorgeous Egyptian actress who starred in Armani Beauty's "Sì Passione Intense" campaign.

"*THE SERIES OF PIECES MR. ARMANI CREATED FOR ME ARE TRULY ICONIC;* THEY REPRESENT NOT ONLY BEAUTIFUL FASHION, BUT MY SPIRIT AND ESSENCE."

ARMANI *is a* RED CARPET STANDOUT

GIORGIO ARMANI was very well known for his close relationships with celebrities who wore his clothing over the years.

M

Maybe it was his close connection to the film industry with all the costume design work that he did, or maybe it was the fact that his magnetic personality drew fabulous friends to him from all over the world. Either way, his clothes were very well represented on the red carpets, at award shows, and present at all kinds of important world events. There is something absolutely phenomenal about wearing an Armani suit or intricate evening gown.

If you name an A-lister in Hollywood, they have probably appeared in photos in something the great Armani has designed. Let's look at some of the most memorable looks over the years that have made Armani one of the greatest designers ever to have dressed the stars as a red carpet standout.

DIANE *KEATON*

THIS APPEARANCE by the late great Diane Keaton at the Academy Awards really heralded the arrival of Armani in Hollywood. Her strong-shouldered jacket over a skirt was not only an unusual woman-wearing-menswear look at the time, but it was pure Diane style and everyone adored her for it. And by proxy, it made Armani's name and marked his beginning as one of the designers to wear on the red carpet. By helping to redefine what a female star could wear, his tailoring was stellar and instead of a traditional gown, he was able to merge masculine and feminine cues. It didn't hurt that she actually won an Oscar that year, so her look was even more noticed on stage during her speech.

JULIA
ROBERTS

AT THE 1990 GOLDEN GLOBES

ANOTHER KILLER EXAMPLE of women rocking a gorgeous menswear look was superstar Julia Roberts at the 1990 Golden Globes. It was a steel-gray Armani suit that turned heads and became an emblem of the era. The bold choice on Julia's part to not wear an evening gown and to help blur gendered fashions on the red carpet, and to reinforce Armani's power in menswear for women, was a huge moment for the Armani brand. She was there as a nominee for Best Supporting Actress for Steel Magnolias. She has said in interviews that this was one of her favorite all-time outfits to wear and that she actually had it tailored at the Giorgio Armani store on Rodeo Drive.

MICHELLE
PFEIFFER

AN AMAZING ACTRESS known for her beauty and uncompromising work in such films as Dangerous Liaisons and Dangerous Minds, one of her best Armani moments was at the 1990 Academy Awards. She wasn't in menswear though; this was a pure Armani gown moment where she wore a sleek, long-sleeve midnight Armani gown with a string of pearls. The look merged timeless glamour with Armani's preference for clean lines and subtle luxury. It stands out as one of the best since it showcases Armani's versatility, not just tailoring for women's suits, but also elevated eveningwear that is pure magic.

SHARON
STONE

AT THE ACADEMY AWARDS IN 1996

THIS LOOK ROCKED the entire fashion world. It was a huge deal that movie star Sharon Stone arrived wearing a long black velvet jacket by Armani rather than a traditional gown. Underneath that, she wore a black turtleneck from the Gap, which was from her own closet rather than a couture dress. This was the ideal mix of luxury with affordability that was genius. The look was finished off with a gardenia pinned to the lapel of the jacket. It was an impromptu look that paired high-low together with gorgeous ease.

ANNE
HATHAWAY

AT THE 2009 ACADEMY AWARDS

THIS WAS A BIG YEAR for Anne, since she was nominated for Rachel Getting Married that year. The gown was a strapless, column-style design in a champagne tone with touches of silver. It was fitted to her body but ended in a mermaid-style skirt that looked like there was a burst of light coming up from beneath her. This dress is often described as one of her best looks and a standout on the red carpet for the Armani brand.

RIHANNA

AT THE 2012 GRAMMY AWARDS

ARMANI DIDN'T JUST DRESS movie stars, but had his hand in adorning the music elite. That included Rihanna at the 2012 Grammy Awards. Armani made her a custom black silk gown which was the exact ideal of what a minimalist evening gown should look like in this elegant, yet understated style. It had a deep plunging neckline down the front with a high slit up the side and a dramatically open back. This was a statement dress like no other. Rihanna looked every bit the pop goddess she truly is in this gown.

CATE
BLANCHETT

AT THE 2018 VENICE FILM FESTIVAL

CATE BLANCHETT CAN really wear anything. She could show up on a red carpet wearing a plastic bag and probably look fantastic. So when she shows up in Armani, and she has maintained a long relationship with the designer, she is going to look her absolute best. That was definitely the case when she appeared at the 2018 Venice Film Festival dressed in Armani Privé. The dress was beyond fabulous with a composition of black silk velvet, floor-length, and had a dramatic plunging sweetheart neckline. She wore it with a feathered capelet, giving it a surreal and ethereal look that was memorable. The press loved the fact that she looked so Old Hollywood glamorous, but with a dress that was made of modern materials.

NICOLE
KIDMAN

AT THE 2018 ACADEMY AWARDS

NICOLE KIDMAN IS ONE of those actresses with a figure that can look incredible in anything she wears. This is especially true of any Armani gown. One such time that she floored the red carpet with her beauty was at the 2018 Academy Awards. The gown was a strapless cobalt blue column dress that had a large sculptural bow at her delicate waist. It also had a high slit on the side of the leg for extra statement drama. She paired the dress with mirrored silver pumps, jewelry by Harry Winston, and a vintage 1953 watch by Omega.

KERI
RUSSELL

AT THE 2025 EMMY AWARDS

AT THE 2025 EMMY AWARDS, one of the standout designs of the night was the Armani dress that Keri Russell wore. In Armani Privé, she wore a design that featured a silk satin oversized bow-shaped bodice and a black velvet skirt. The neckline had a plunging effect and there was a subtle mesh cut-out with crystal patterning under the bow detail. The look was widely interpreted as a tribute to the late Giorgio Armani, who had passed away ten days earlier, by choosing Armani on such a big night.

"I STILL HAVE A CLOSET FULL OF THOSE BEAUTIFUL SUITS, THOSE CLASSIC SUITS, *AND I STILL WEAR THEM.*"

Glenn Close to People.com

ARMANI *Without* THE MAN HIMSELF

The Future

AS DISCUSSED IN THE FIRST CHAPTER, Giorgio Armani, one of the greatest fashion designers ever, passed away September 4, 2025, at the age of 91. His memory lives on through his family, his many famous friends, and the gorgeous clothing he designed for over 50 years.

ne of the ways the company and his family intend to honor his legacy is through the Armani/Archivo. It's a celebration of his life's work
and the man himself. This is a project to catalogue, digitize, preserve,
and share five decades of the brand's creative output. It aims to preserve thousands of garments, looks, accessories, sketches, and images from the brand's history from about 1975 to the present.
An interpretation of heritage not as something static, but as "living
material" that connects past, present, and future. There is a physi-
cal/experiential dimension of clothing on display, along with digital
access. The archives will be shown via boutiques, exhibitions, loca-
tion-specific selections, and archival pieces being re-issued or made
available in various global cities. It's truly the most glorious way to
celebrate everything Giorgio Armani did throughout his life and ca-
reer.

There are so many benefits to the Armani/Archivo for fashion fans
around the world. It supports themes of sustainability and circular-
ity. The archive isn't just "old stuff locked away," but pieces that can
be re-interpreted, re-issued, circulated, and thereby reduce waste or
reinforce longevity. So it helps to contribute to the company's belief
in getting away from fast fashion and having sustainable goals.
For researchers, fashion students, fans, and professionals, it be-
comes a resource to understand the design codes, evolution of materials, silhouettes, and the brand identity of Armani over time. It aims
to make Armani's substantial fashion legacy timeless and forever,
even if the man himself has passed on.

MUSEUM
Armani/Silos is Giorgio
Armani's Milan exhibition
space, presenting fashion,
art, photography, and de-
sign narratives globally.

AT HOME
Giorgio Armani poses
during Milan Fashion
Week in 2016.

he start of the project kicked off at the Venice International Film Festival in August 2025. The archive pieces will then travel to major cities in curated forms, including Milan, Paris, London, Los Angeles, New York, Beijing, and Tokyo. One of the most important stops was, of course, Milan, at a public exhibition of about 150 looks, which was staged at the Pinacoteca di Brera in the famed Italian city during Fashion Week. Each item is a testimony of a creative gesture, with every detail revealing the evolution and consistency of forms, materials, silhouettes, and the intentions of this great designer. His coherent style and vision developed over decades is how that legacy can inform future creation by keeping the Armani/Archivo alive and well.

Keep in mind the Armani/Archivo features clothing from over 200 collections with over 30,000 pieces represented. The true magnitude

Giorgio Armani and Leo dell'Orco at a basketball game in Milan.

of this collection is mind-blowing when you think about how it stands for the countless hours and years of work. The future of Armani as a worldwide fashion phenomenon is definitely guaranteed.

At the helm of the Armani corporation now, in October 2025, the Armani Group announced that Giuseppe Marsocci, a 23-year veteran of the company and former global chief commercial officer, became CEO. He will report to the Board of Directors, which is chaired by Leo Dell'Orco, Giorgio Armani's longtime partner and collaborator. His succession plan allocated 40 percent of the voting rights to be in the hands of Leo.

The leadership change reflects a strategy of choosing executives from within the brand who know its DNA well rather than bringing in a complete outsider. The ownership structure is designed to balance family and partner control, institutional oversight (via the Foundation), and potential external investment via the stake sale. The preferred-buyer clause underscores a desire to grow or partner strategically while preserving brand identity (rather than a forced sale to just any buyer). The CEO's role now combines maintaining the "Armani aesthetic" and heritage with adapting to changes in luxury: global demand shifts, evolving consumer habits, and retail disruptions.

"HE DRESSED ME FOR SO MANY TURNING POINTS IN MY LIFE. HE SHAPED NOT JUST HOW WE DRESS, BUT HOW WE FEEL."

Sharon Stone to AP.

WOMEN'S CANCER
RESEARCH FUND
RESEARCH FOUNDATION PROGRAM
#WCRFCURE
WOMEN'S CANCER
RESEARCH FUND
CANCER RESEARCH FOUNDATION PROGRAM
#WCRFCURE
WOMEN
RESEAR
A BREAST CANCER RESEARCH
WOMEN
RESEAR
A BREAST CAN
#WCRF
#WCRFCURE

CREDITS

Helmin Publishing would like to thank the following
for permission to use images in this book.

7	FashionStock.com	Shutterstock.com
8	ARCHIVIO GBB	Alamy.com
9	Real_life_photo	Shutterstock.com
11	Valentina Linnik	
12	Valentina Linnik	
15	chris87	Shutterstock.com
19		Shutterstock.com
20	Independent Photo Agency	Alamy Live News
21	Paul Smith	Featureflash
23	s_bukley	Shutterstock.com
25	Everett Collection	Shutterstock.com
29	Harsh	Shutterstock.com
30	Glasshouse Images	Alamy
31	Allstar Picture Library Limited	Alamy
32	Independent Photo Agency Srl	Alamy
33	FashionStock.com	Shutterstock.com
34		Shutterstock.com
35	BalazsSebok	Shutterstock.com
36	T Fabrizio Andrea Bertani	Shutterstock.com
36	M	Shutterstock.com
36	B Ev. Safronov	Shutterstock.com
38	Featureflash Photo Agency	Shutterstock.com
42	FashionStock.com	Shutterstock.com
43	FashionStock.com	Shutterstock.com
44	Valentina Linnik	
45	Louise WateridgeZUMA Wire	Alamy Live News
46	Featureflash Photo Agency	Shutterstock.com
48	Valentina Linnik	
50	andersphoto	Shutterstock.com
52	taniavolobueva	Shutterstock.com
57	K I Photography	Shutterstock.com
60	Valentina Linnik	
61	Valentina Linnik	
63	Lorraine Traynor	Alamy.com

64	Michael Potts F1	Shutterstock.com
68	photo-lime	Shutterstock.com
70	Valentina	Linnik
77	FashionStock.com	Shutterstock.com
81	Strikernia	Shutterstock.com
82	T RGR Collection	Alamy.com
82	BR DACFILM Rome	Album
82	BL Collection Christophel	Alamy.com
85	Joe Seer	Shutterstock.com
89	UPIJim Ruymen	Alamy.com
90	Globe Photos	ZUMAPRESS.com
93	Featureflash Photo Agency	Shutterstock.com
97	FashionStock.com	Shutterstock.com
101	FashionStock.com	
103	Globe Photos	ZUMAPRESS.com
111	Tinseltown	Shutterstock.com
112	Andrea Raffin	Shutterstock.com
117	Fred Duval	Shutterstock.com
119	Globe Photos	ZUMAPRESS.com
120	Ralph Dominguez	MediaPunch
121	Ralph Dominguez	MediaPunch
122	Globe Photos	ZUMAPRESS.com
124	Featureflash Photo Agency	Shutterstock.com
125	Featureflash Photo Agency	Shutterstock.com
127	Andrea Raffin	Shutterstock.com
128	Tinseltown	Shutterstock.com
131	UPI	Alamy Live News
133	Featureflash Photo Agency	Shutterstock.com
136	Charlotte ten Haave	Shutterstock.com
137	T photo-lime	Shutterstock.com
137	B DELBO ANDREA	Shutterstock.com
38	Independent Photo Agency	Alamy Live News
139	photo-lime	Shutterstock.com
141	DFree	Shutterstock.com

Helmin Publishing, 2026
Nivå Strandpark 21, 1
DK-2990 Nivå
Denmark

TEXT: Kelly Reising
DESIGN: butter am brot

ISBN: 97887-85374-18-9

Printet at Print Best, Estonia, 2026
1. edition, 1. printing